MAKE QUICKBOOKS
DCAA COMPLIANT

MAKE QUICKBOOKS DCAA COMPLIANT

DCAA ToolKit - Module 2

C. P. KRISHNAN

Copyright © 2016 **C. P. Krishnan**
All rights reserved
ISBN-13: 9781533140258
ISBN-10:1533140251

No part of this publication may be reproduced, stored in any retrieval system, or transmitted in any form or electronic, mechanical, photocopying, recording, scanning, or otherwise, except as permitted under Section 107 or Section 108 of the 1976 United States Copyright Act, without prior written approval of the Author.

Limit of Liability/Disclamier of Warranty: While the author has used his/her best efforts in compiling & preparing the material presented, they make no representations or warranties express or implied with regard to the accuracy or completeness of the contents of this book. The authors disclaim any warranties express or implied to the merchantabilityor fitness for a particular purpose. The reader should consult with professional experts when appropriate. The author(s) and CAK International shall not be liable for any financial loss, commercial damages, including but not limited to special, incidental, consequential or other damages.

> "Wisdom is the principal thing;
> therefore get **wisdom**: and
> with all thy getting
> get **understanding**"
>
> (PROVERBS 4:7)

Words cannot express the special Thanks to my parents who have dedicated their lives to make mine better. Without their love, faith, and support none of this would be possible.

IMPORTANT

As with all print & media material - this book and the entire collective DCAA Toolkit is not to be construed in any manner as the authority in the subject matters discussed herewith. The Federal Acquisition Regulations (FAR), DFARS, and the DCAA Contract Audit Manual (CAM) are the sole sources for authority statements and regulations. This material is for CAS Exempt contracts only.

Any and all claims made in this collective DCAA Toolkit effort are offered simply as a consultative guide towards the process of becoming compliant in selective areas. Compliance is a broad term that includes more than just accounting systems, policies etc., and the Administrative Contracting Officer (ACO) & DCAA/DCMA alone can render that decision. The DCAA/DCMA alone is the final authority and in no manner does any material present herewith guarantee compliance – that decision rest with the DCAA and the DCMA alone. No information rendered in this collective DCAA Toolkit is a statement made by an officer of law, attorney, or other legally represented individual or organization and all liabilities resulting from the usage or reliance on any contents solely rest with the buyer/subscriber of this material and not with the author(s) or CAK International, LLC.

The government has developed manuals, archives, memorandums and other material to support and implement the regulations outlined. Reference material as detailed in this collective DCAA Toolkit® is available at www.dcaa.mil, www.acquisition.gov. and http://www.acq.osd.mil.

INTRODUCTION

This collective DCAA Toolkit is another step of its author Mr. C. P. Krishnan (CP) towards adding value to the Small Business Contracting community. Since the Year 1999 CP has been serving as one of the Senior Partners at CAK International, LLC. **CAK** provides customized business solutions to promote and develop successful companies based on Biblical Principles.

We understand the strain Government contractors are placed upon to pass the Defense Contract Audit Agency (DCAA) audits. In some cases, this comes down to solvency and resource reduction if the audits are not passed. This collective DCAA Toolkit (3 Modules) contains proven, actual, and real time valuable insights that can be incorporated to achieve and maintain DCAA compliance.

CP holds advanced educational qualifications including Certifications in Accounting & Auditing, Certified QuickBooks Pro Advisor, Certified Cost & Associate Chartered Accountant, Masters in Business Administration (MBA), Certified FISMA & ITAR Specialist, and is certified as a Specialist in Sarbanes Oxley Compliance (CSOX) & Corporate Governance. CP along with the CAK team is actively involved in presenting Subject Matter seminars through multiple district offices and chapters of the U.S. Small Business Administration, SCORE, SBDC, WBC, CDCs, local Universities, IEEE, and at notable Conferences.

We believe in making the DCAA and the Small Business Contractor's job a little easier in the national interest of our United States government. I personally thank you and sincerely hope that this collective DCAA ToolKit delivers valuable information in the path to compliance.

Blessings,

C. P. Krishnan

TABLE OF CONTENTS

	Important · vii
	Introduction · ix
	Please Note · xiii
Chapter 1	Pre-Award Accounting Systems Audit · · · · · · · · · · · · · 1
Chapter 2	Pre-Award Survey of Prospective Contractor's Accounting System Checklist· 9
Chapter 3	FAR 16.3013 Requirement ·25
Chapter 4	Chart of Accounts ·27
	Sample Chart of Accounts – DCAA Compliant · · · · · · ·29
	- Keys to Compliant DCAA Chart of Accounts · · · · · · 48
Chapter 5	Item Listing· ·49
Chapter 6	Customer Profiles ·53
Chapter 7	Payroll & Timekeeping ·59
Chapter 8	Invoicing and Booked vs. Billed· · · · · · · · · · · · · · · · · ·65
Chapter 9	Accounting Best Practices for Compliance· · · · · · · · · · ·71
	More from CAK International, LLC · · · · · · · · · · · · · · ·85

PLEASE NOTE

Module 2 of the DCAA Toolkit "How to make QuickBooks DCAA Compliant" includes a one-time download of an Compliant Chart of Accounts (COA) by visiting **www.cakintl.com/ebooks** and following the instructions on the screen. Be advised that you follow the directions very carefully as downloadable errors caused by any software, hardware, and/or operator issues will not be honored by the author and the company.

This is to ensure copyright protection and preventing piracy of protected material.

Chapter 1

PRE-AWARD ACCOUNTING SYSTEMS AUDIT

One of the first steps in the Pre-Award Audit is to evaluate the design of Accounting System to determine if it is acceptable for a prospective contract. DCAA or Buying Command will request that the contractor complete an Accounting System Checklist. Contractor should be prepared to demonstrate how the accounting system satisfies SF 1408 criteria at initial meeting.

AFTER CONTRACT AWARD

DFARS 252.242-7006 (a) (1) Defines an Acceptable Accounting System as a system that complies with the reasonable assurance that:

* Applicable laws and regulations are complied with;
* The accounting system and cost data are reliable;
* Risk of misallocations and mischarges are minimized; and
* Contract allocations and charges are consistent with billing procedures

ACCOUNTING SYSTEM

DFARS 252.242-7006 (a) (2) defines a "Contractor's system or systems for accounting methods, procedures, and controls established to gather, record, classify, analyze, summarize, interpret, and present accurate and timely financial data for reporting in compliance with applicable laws, regulations, and management decisions". May include subsystems for specific areas such as:

* Billing
* Labor

TOTAL CONTRACT COSTS

DFARS 252.242-7006(c)(2) requires "Proper segregation of direct costs from indirect costs." The total cost of a contract is the sum of the direct and indirect costs allocable to the contract. While the total cost of a contract includes all costs properly allocable to the contract, the allowable costs to the Government are limited to those allocable costs which are allowable pursuant to Part 31 and applicable agency supplements.

DIRECT COST

DFARS 252.242-7006 (c)(3) requires Identification and accumulation of direct costs by contract; FAR 2.101 Defines Direct Cost as "any cost that is identified specifically with a particular final cost objective." Direct costs are not limited to items that are incorporated in the end product as material or labor. No **final cost objective** shall have **allocated** to it as a direct cost any cost that has been included in an **indirect cost pool**. Direct costs of the contract shall be charged directly to the contract.

INDIRECT COST

Indirect cost means any cost not directly identified with a single, final cost objective, but identified with two or more final cost objectives or an intermediate cost objective. DFARS 252.242-7006 (c)(4) requires "A logical and consistent method for the accumulation and allocation of indirect costs to intermediate and final cost objectives".

The term indirect cost covers a wide variety of cost categories and the costs involved are not all incurred for the same reasons. The number of indirect cost accounts in a single company can range from one to hundreds. The indirect structure needs to be tailored to your company and how it operates. In general, indirect cost accounts fall into two broad categories:

* Overhead
* General and Administrative

Overhead Cost. Examples of indirect cost rates include:

* Material overhead
* Manufacturing overhead
* Engineering overhead
* Site overhead

General & Administrative Cost. These are management, financial, and other expenses related to the general management and administration of the business as a whole. To be considered a G&A Expense, the expenditure must be incurred by, or allocated to, the general business unit. Examples of G&A expenses include:

* Salary and other costs of the executive staff of the corporate or home office
* Salary and other costs of staff services as legal, accounting, public relations, etc.
* Selling and marketing expenses

ALLOCATION BASE

Indirect costs should be allocated based on benefits accrued to intermediate and final cost objectives.

* Allocation base must be reasonable.
* There must be a relationship between the selected allocation base and the pool costs.

For example, training costs in the overhead pool are not necessarily caused by a particular cost objective, but the cost objectives might benefit from the training of employees. In that case, training would be related and benefit the labor dollars incurred on contracts/final cost objective.

TYPICAL ALLOCATION BASES ARE:

OVERHEAD:
Direct Labor Dollars
Direct Labor Hours
Direct Material Dollars

G&A:
Total Cost Input: (Total direct and indirect costs minus G&A)
Value Added: (TCI less subcontracts, and direct materials)
Single Cost Element: (e.g. Direct labor dollars)

ALLOWABILITY

FAR 31.201-2 defines that a cost is allowable only when the cost complies with all of the following requirements:

* Reasonableness
* Allocability

* Terms of the Contract
* Applicable Cost Accounting Standards (CAS)
* Any Limitations Set forth in the entire Subpart 31.201

REASONABLENESS

FAR 31.201-3 defines a cost to be reasonable if in its nature and amount, it does not exceed that which would be incurred by a prudent person in the conduct of competitive business. It is the contractor's responsibility to establish that each cost is reasonable.

ALLOCABILITY

FAR 31.201-4 defines a cost is allocable to a government contract if it:

* Is incurred specifically for the contract;
* Benefits both the contract and other work, and can be distributed to them in reasonable proportion to the benefits received; or
* Is necessary to the overall operation of the business, although a direct relationship to any particular cost objective cannot be shown

CONTRACT TERMS

Specific types of cost are often addressed in a contract or request for proposal (RFP). However, the contract terms can only be more restrictive than the other factors that must be considered in determining cost allowability, not less. In other words, the contract terms cannot allow a cost that is:

* Unreasonable
* Improperly measured, assigned and allocated to the contract
* Unallowable in accordance with specific cost principles

ACCOUNTING FOR CONTRACT COSTS

The accounting system must be able to accumulate and report the costs for each final cost objective; i.e. government contract.

DIRECT CONTRACT COSTS + (PLUS) ALLOCATION OF INDIRECT COSTS – (MINUS) UNALLOWABLE COSTS

DFARS 252.242-7006 (c) requirements:

* Accumulation of costs under general ledger control
* Reconciliation of subsidiary cost ledgers and cost objectives to general ledger
* Approval and documentation of adjusting entries
* Interim (at least monthly) determination of costs charged to a contract through routine posting of books of accounts

LABOR SYSTEM

DFARS 252.242-7006 (c) requirements:

* A timekeeping system that identifies employees' labor by intermediate or final cost objectives
* A labor distribution system that charges direct and indirect labor to the appropriate cost objectives
* Labor should be charged to intermediate and final cost objectives based on a timekeeping document (paper or electronic timecards) completed and certified by the employees and approved by the employees' supervisors.
* Employees should fill out timesheet on a daily basis and include all hours worked including Uncompensated Overtime.
* Labor cost distribution records should be reconcilable to payroll records and labor distribution records should trace to and from the job cost ledger and general ledger accounts.

UNALLOWABLE COSTS

DFARS 252.242-7006 (c) (12) requires "Exclusion from costs charged to Government contracts of amounts which are not allowable in terms of Federal Acquisition Regulation (FAR) part 31, Contract Cost Principles and Procedures, and other contract provisions;".

* Contractors need <u>written</u> policies and procedures (provided in DCAA Compliance Kit Module 3) to identify and exclude unallowable costs.
* Unallowable costs need to be identified and excluded from any billings, claims, and proposals applicable to a Government contract

COSTS BY CONTRACT LINE ITEM

DFARS 252.242-7006 (c)(13) requires "Identification of costs by contract line item and by units (as if each unit or line item were a separate contract), if required by the contract". Therefore, the accounting system needs to be able to expand beyond a Project Number. Each job needs to be expanded to the requisite level of detail as determined by contract terms.

BILLINGS

DFARS 252.242-7006 (c)(16) requirements:

* Billings that can be reconciled to the cost accounts for both current and cumulative amounts claimed and comply with contract terms
* Contractors should only bill cost which comply with FAR 52.216-7
* Recorded costs that have been paid by cash, check, or other form of actual payment for items or services purchased directly for the contract
* When the Contractor is not delinquent in paying costs of contract performance in the ordinary course of business, costs incurred, but not necessarily paid, for supplies and services purchased directly for

the contract and associated financing payments to subcontractors, provided payments due will be made:
* In accordance with the terms and conditions of a subcontract or invoice; and
* Ordinarily within 30 days of the submission of the Contractor's payment request to the Government

* Billings need to be based on current contract provisions. The total amount billed should not exceed any contract, work order, funding limitation, or any contract ceiling
* Important to brief contract to identify billing provisions, including but not limited to:
  * Restriction of billing frequency
  * Special withholding provisions
  * Contractual unallowable costs
  * A contractor needs to reconcile booked costs to billed costs.

COST ACCOUNTING INFORMATION

DFARS 252.242-7006 (c) requires Cost accounting information, as required:

* By contract clauses concerning limitation of cost (FAR 52.232-20), limitation of funds (FAR 52.232-22), or allowable cost and payment (FAR 52.216-7)
* To readily calculate indirect cost rates from the books of accounts
* Interim rates should be routinely monitored. At least monthly, an employee needs to be responsible for monitoring total contract expenditure against contract limitations on price or cost.
* Adequate, reliable data for use in pricing follow-on acquisitions
* Accounting practices in accordance with standards promulgated by the Cost Accounting Standards Board, If applicable otherwise - Generally Accepted Accounting Principles (GAAP).

Chapter 2

PRE-AWARD SURVEY OF PROSPECTIVE CONTRACTOR'S ACCOUNTING SYSTEM CHECKLIST

PRE-AWARD SURVEY (SF 1408) OF PROSPECTIVE CONTRACTOR ACCOUNTING SYSTEM

Date: XX/XX/201X

Company Name, Contract Number, and **Full Address**:	Click here to enter
Commercial and Government Agency (CAGE) Code Number: (found at http://www.dlis.dla.mil/cage_welcome.asp)	Click here to enter
Data Universal Numbering System (DUNS) Number: (FAR 52.204-6)	Click here to enter
Cognizant Defense Contract Audit Agency (DCAA) office info (Address / ph # / /email) – (found at http://www.dcaa.mil/office_locator.html)	Click here to enter text.
Company Point of Contact: (Name, Title, Phone Number, and E-mail address)	Click here to enter

www.cakintl.com/dcaa

Name, Title, and Signature of Company Principal (President / VP / Controller, etc.) responsible for the design of the Accounting System.

Name

Title

Email Address

Signature

Make QuickBooks DCAA Compliant

SF1408

PLEASE ANSWER QUESTIONS BELOW:

HAVE YOU READ THE REQUIREMENTS IN THE SF1408? (YES/NO)

HAVE YOU READ THE DCAA PUBLICATION 7641.90 - "Information for Contractors" ON DCAA's WEBSITE at http://www.dcaa.mil/? (YES/NO)

For each Question, check only one box. ALL Questions must have explanatory narrative text entered in the boxes. Please provide sufficient detail to describe the process (Including Account Numbers / Process Flow etc.). Each Question must be complete. Do NOT refer to previous answers, (i.e. "See Question 3 Above").

1. Has your organization's <u>Accounting</u> System ever been audited by DCAA?

YES (if YES, attach a copy of their most recent DCAA audit report to this Modified Pre-Award Survey) or provide DCAA Report # or DCAA POC info.

NO (if NO, answer N/A to Questions 1.A., 1.B., and 1.C. below)

1.A. If the answer is "Yes" to Question 1 above, when was the audit performed?

Within the past 1 Year. Within the past 3 Years.
Greater than 3 Years (PROVIDE THE YEAR THE AUDIT WAS PERFORMED - _____).

N/A (Answer to Question 1 is NO)

SF1408

1.B. If the answer is "Yes" to Question 1 above, did DCAA determine the Accounting System acceptable for award of prospective contracts?

YES

NO (if NO provide an explanation in the box below)

N/A (Answer to Question 1 is NO)

> Enter Text Here

1.C. If the answer is "Yes" to Question 1 above, have there been any changes to the Accounting System since the DCAA audit?

YES (if YES, describe the changes in the box below)

NO

N/A (Answer to Question 1 is NO)

> Enter Text Here

SF1408

2. Is your organization subject to CAS (48 CFR Chapter 99)?

YES (If YES, is it FULL or MODIFIED CAS?)   FULL   MODIFIED

(If YES (FULL or MODIFIED), the Offeror <u>MUST</u> attach a copy of their most recent audit reports/documentation regarding all CAS compliance or non-compliance issues to this Modified Pre-Award Survey)

NO (if NO, provide an explanation in the box below why your organization is exempt and answer N/A to Questions 2.A., 2.B., and 2.C. below)

> Enter Text Here

2.A. Has your organization submitted a CASB disclosure statement (CASB DS-1) to DCAA and has it been determined adequate?

YES (if YES, provide an explanation that <u>validates</u> your answer in the box below)

NO (if NO, provide an explanation in the box below)

N/A (Answer to Question 2 is NO)

> Enter Text Here

SF1408

2.B. Has your organization been notified by DCAA that it is in (or may be in) noncompliance with its disclosure statement or CAS?

YES (if YES, provide an explanation that <u>validates</u> your answer in the box below)

NO (if NO, provide an explanation in the box below)

N/A (N/A, if the answer to Question 2 is NO)

> Enter Text Here

2.C. Is any aspect of this proposal inconsistent with your organization's disclosed practices or applicable CAS?

YES (if YES, provide an explanation that <u>validates</u> your answer in the box below)

NO (if NO, provide an explanation in the box below)

N/A (N/A, if the answer to Question 2 is NO or if you have no current, active proposal being considered)

> Enter Text Here

SF1408

Instruction: If the Contractor is planning on bidding on Cost Type Contracts, the contractor MUST provide explanatory narrative for all of the following questions:

3. Has your organization's Accounting System been audited by an outside Certified Public Accountant/Consultant or other Cognizant Federal Agency other than DCAA?

YES (If YES, the Offeror MUST attach a copy of their most recent audit report to this Modified Pre- Award Survey) NOTE: Do not submit your Annual Financial Audit.

NO

4. Is your organization's Accounting System currently in full operation?

YES (if YES, provide an explanation that validates your answer in the box below)

NO (if NO, provide an explanation in the box below which portions are (1) in operation, (2) set up, but not yet in operation, (3) anticipated, or (4) non-existent)

N/A (if N/A, provide an explanation in the box below)

> Enter Text Here

www.cakintl.com/dcaa

SF1408

5. Is your organization's Accounting System in accord with Generally Accepted Accounting Principles (GAAP) Applicable in the Circumstances?

YES (if YES, provide an explanation that <u>validates</u> your answer in the box below)

NO (if NO, provide an explanation in the box below)

N/A (if N/A, provide an explanation in the box below)

> Enter Text Here

6. Is your organization's Accounting System ready for a DCAA audit?

YES (if YES, provide an explanation that <u>validates</u> your answer in the box below)

NO (if NO, provide an explanation in the box below as to when you will be ready for an Audit)

N/A (if N/A, provide an explanation in the box below)

> Enter Text Here

SF1408

7. Are the loaded hourly labor rates proposed consistent with your established estimating and accounting principles and procedures and FAR Part 31, Cost Principles? (Answer this Question "N/A" if you do not have an active proposal)

YES (if YES, provide an explanation that validates your answer in the box below)

NO (if NO, provide an explanation in the box below)

N/A (if N/A, provide an explanation in the box below)

> Enter Text Here

8. Does the Accounting System provide for the proper segregation of Direct Costs from Indirect Costs?

YES (if YES, provide an explanation that validates your answer in the box below)

NO (if NO, provide an explanation in the box below)

N/A (if N/A, provide an explanation in the box below)

> Enter Text Here

SF1408

9. Does the Accounting System provide for the identification and accumulation of Direct Costs by contract?

YES (if YES, provide an explanation that <u>validates</u> your answer in the box below)

NO (if NO, provide an explanation in the box below)

N/A (if N/A, provide an explanation in the box below)

> Enter Text Here

10. Does the Accounting System provide for a logical and consistent method for the allocation of Indirect Costs to intermediate and final cost objectives? (A contract is a final cost objective.)

YES (if YES, provide an explanation that <u>validates</u> your answer in the box below)

NO (if NO, provide an explanation in the box below)

N/A (if N/A, provide an explanation in the box below)

> Enter Text Here

SF1408

11. Does the Accounting System provide for the accumulation of costs under general ledger control?

YES (if YES, provide an explanation that <u>validates</u> your answer in the box below)

NO (if NO, provide an explanation in the box below)

N/A (if N/A, provide an explanation in the box below)

> Enter Text Here

12. Does the Accounting System provide for a timekeeping system that identifies employees' labor by intermediate or final cost objectives?

YES (if YES, provide an explanation that <u>validates</u> your answer in the box below)

NO (if NO, provide an explanation in the box below)

> Enter Text Here

SF1408

13. Does the Accounting System provide for a labor distribution system that charges Direct and Indirect labor to the appropriate cost objectives?

YES (if YES, provide an explanation that <u>validates</u> your answer in the box below)

NO (if NO, provide an explanation in the box below)

> Enter Text Here

14. Does the Accounting System provide for an interim (at least monthly) determination of costs charged to a contract through routine posting of books of account?

YES (if YES, provide an explanation that <u>validates</u> your answer in the box below)

NO (if NO, provide an explanation in the box below)

> Enter Text Here

SF1408

15. Does the Accounting System provide for an exclusion of costs charged to government contracts of amounts which are not allowable in terms of FAR 31, Contract Cost Principles and Procedures, or other contract provisions?

YES (if YES, provide an explanation that <u>validates</u> your answer in the box below)

NO (if NO, provide an explanation in the box below)

> Enter Text Here

16. Does the Accounting System provide for the identification of costs by contract line item and by units (as if each unit or line item were a separate contract) if required by the proposed contract?

YES (if YES, provide an explanation that <u>validates</u> your answer in the box below)

NO (if NO, provide an explanation in the box below)

> Enter Text Here

SF1408

17. Does the Accounting System provide for the segregation of preproduction costs from production costs?

YES (if YES, provide an explanation that <u>validates</u> your answer in the box below)

NO (if NO, provide an explanation in the box below)

> Enter Text Here

18. Does the Accounting System provide financial information as required by contract clauses concerning Limitation of Cost (FAR 52.232-20 and 21) or Limitation on Payments (FAR 52.216-16)?

YES (if YES, provide an explanation that <u>validates</u> your answer in the box below)

NO (if NO, provide an explanation in the box below)

> Enter Text Here

SF1408

19. Does the Accounting System provide financial information required to support requests for Progress Payments?

YES (if YES, provide an explanation that <u>validates</u> your answer in the box below)

NO (if NO, provide an explanation in the box below)

> Enter Text Here

20. Is the Accounting System designed, and are the records maintained, in such a manner that adequate, reliable data are developed for use in pricing follow-on acquisitions?

YES (if YES, provide an explanation that <u>validates</u> your answer in the box below)

NO (if NO, provide an explanation in the box below)

> Enter Text Here

SF1408

21. Is your organization planning on submitting proposals on Cost-Type (FAR 16.3) contracts/task orders?

YES

NO (if NO, provide an explanation in the box below)

> Enter Text Here

22. Is your organization currently performing on Cost-Type (FAR 16.3) contracts/task orders?

YES

NO

> Enter Text Here

Chapter 3

FAR 16.3013 REQUIREMENT

"Requires that a contractor's accounting system be adequate for determining costs applicable to the contract prior to the award of a cost reimbursable contract, grant, SBIR, or BAA. An adequate accounting system is not an evaluation criterion. It is a basic contract requirement with a pass/fail determination."

"A contract vehicle may only be awarded to an offeror who is determined to have an adequate accounting system by the Defense Contract Audit Agency (DCAA)."

Core elements of an Adequate Accounting System:

* Conforms with Generally Accepted Accounting Principles (GAAP)
* Produces Equitable Results that are Verifiable
* Applicable to the Contemplated Contract(s)
* Is capable of being Consistently Followed
* Proper Segregation of Direct costs from Indirect costs
* Identification and accumulation of Direct costs by Contract
* A logical and consistent method for allocation of Indirect costs to Intermediate and Final cost objectives

* Accumulation of costs under General Ledger control
* A timekeeping system that identifies employees' labor by Intermediate or Final Cost objectives
* A labor distribution system that charges direct and indirect labor to the appropriate cost objectives
* Interim (at least monthly) determination of costs charged to a contract through routine posting to books of account
* Exclusion from costs charged to Government contracts of amounts that are not allowable pursuant to Federal Acquisition Regulation (FAR) Part 31, Contract Cost Principles and Procedures, or other contract provisions
* Identification of costs by contract line item and units by the proposed contract
* Segregation of preproduction costs from production costs

WHY ACCOUNTING SYSTEMS FAIL:

* Unallowable costs not accounted for separately
* No cumulative labor distribution and/or job cost ledgers
* No written policies and procedures

Chapter 4

CHART OF ACCOUNTS

The main basis of any accounting system is housed in the Chart of Accounts. The Chart of Accounts is a listing of General Ledger accounts used to post transactions into a system. They are grouped by Account Type such as Assets, Liabilities etc. The key difference in a DCAA version vs. non DCAA version is based on the purpose.

Chart of Accounts are more than just simple accounts to categorize transactions to, they serve multiple key purposes as follows:

* They allow for segregation of transactions by categories
* They allow for grouping & sub grouping to create meaningful reports
* They dictate conventional accounting principles to the system based on GAAP
* They help reporting simple for taxation purposes
* They assist management in making strategic business decisions

When it comes to DCAA in addition to the above mentioned benefits they also allow for:

* Cost Accumulation per Government Accounting standards
* Segregate 'unallowed costs' on the General Ledger

* Separate Direct from Indirect Costs
* Create Cost Pools for simpler Indirect Rate calculations

If one word can be used to describe the primary design of a Compliant Chart of Accounts it would be Cost Accumulation by Pools based on DCAA & FAR regulations.

If you are starting to set up your system right now, then it is highly recommended that you use the provided Chart of Accounts format listed in the following pages. If this is an existing system that you are converting, follow the steps of exporting and refining the Chart of Accounts.

Sample Chart of Accounts – DCAA Compliant

Visit www.cakintl.com/ebooks and receive a FREE electronic copy of this file

Acct #	Account Name	Type
10100	Cash on Hand	Bank
11100	Checking Acct	Bank
11400	Savings Acct	Bank
13100	Accounts Receivable	Accounts Receivable
14100	Prepaid Expenses	Other Current Asset
14300	Prepaid Interest	Other Current Asset
14400	Prepaid Taxes	Other Current Asset
14500	Undeposited Funds	Other Current Asset
15000	Inventory	Other Current Asset
16100	Equipment-Office/Admin	Fixed Asset
16110	Acc Depreciation Eqpt Off	Fixed Asset
16200	Equipment -Engineering	Fixed Asset
16210	Acc Depreciation Eqpt Eng	Fixed Asset
16300	Equipment- Testing	Fixed Asset
16310	Acc Depr Eqpt Testing	Fixed Asset
16400	Other Depreciable Prop	Fixed Asset
16410	Acc Depr Other Property	Fixed Asset
16500	Leasehold Improvements	Fixed Asset
16510	Acc Depr Leasehold	Fixed Asset
16600	Software	Fixed Asset
16610	Acc Depr - Software	Fixed Asset
16700	Intellectual Property	Fixed Asset
16800	IRAD Assets	Fixed Asset
16810	Accum Depr-IRAD Assets	Fixed Asset
17000	Cost and Est. Earnings in Excess	Other Asset
18100	Other Assets	Other Asset
18500	Security Deposits	Other Asset

www.cakintl.com/dcaa

Sample Chart of Accounts – DCAA Compliant

Acct #	Account Name	Type
21100	Accounts Payable	Accounts Payable
21200	Checking Acct	Credit Card
21400	Accrued Expenses	Other Current Liability
21401	Accrued Exp:21401 · Accrued Income Taxes Payable	Other Current Liability
21404	Accrued Exp:21404 · Accrued Vacation	Other Current Liability
21406	Accrued Exp:21406 · Accrued Payroll	Other Current Liability
21500	Sales Tax Payable	Other Current Liability
21700	Billings in Excess of Costs	Other Current Liability
24000	Payroll Liabilities	Other Current Liability
25100	Deferred Revenue	Other Current Liability
25200	Advance from Customers	Other Current Liability
27000	Deferred Federal Tax	Long Term Liability
27010	Deferred State Tax	Long Term Liability
30000	Opening Balance Equity	Equity
38000	Paid in Capital	Equity
39000	Retained Earnings	Equity
40000	Revenue	Income
41100	Revenue:41100 · Fixed Price Contract Inc	Income
41300	Revenue:41300 · Cost Reimburse Contr Inc	Income
41301	Revenue:41300 · Cost Reimburse Contr Inc:41301 · Fee Income	Income
41400	Revenue:41400 · Direct Product Sales	Income
41500	Revenue:41500 · Cost Plus Contract Income	Income
41700	Revenue:41700 · Indefinite Del/Qty Contr	Income
41900	Revenue:41900 · T&M Letter Contract Inc	Income
43100	Revenue:43100 · Commercial	Income
43200	Revenue:43200 · Direct Service Sales	Income
44100	Revenue:44100 · Interest Income	Income

Sample Chart of Accounts – DCAA Compliant

Acct #	Account Name	Type
45100	Revenue:45100 · Other Income	Income
47100	Revenue:47100 · Sales Returns and Allow	Income
47200	Revenue:47200 · Sales Discounts	Income
50000	Cost of Goods Sold	Cost of Goods Sold
50100	Cost of Goods Sold:50100 · Direct Labor (Cost Reimb) Wages	Cost of Goods Sold
50110	Cost of Goods Sold:50110 · Direct Labor Other Wages	Cost of Goods Sold
50450	Cost of Goods Sold:50450 · Purchased items	Cost of Goods Sold
50550	Cost of Goods Sold:50550 · Purchased Services	Cost of Goods Sold
50650	Cost of Goods Sold:50650 · Subcontracts	Cost of Goods Sold
50750	Cost of Goods Sold:50750 · Equipment	Cost of Goods Sold
50800	Cost of Goods Sold:50800 · Other Direct Costs	Cost of Goods Sold
50900	Cost of Goods Sold:50900 · Travel	Cost of Goods Sold
50910	Cost of Goods Sold:50900 · Travel:50910 · Airfare	Cost of Goods Sold
50920	Cost of Goods Sold:50900 · Travel:50920 · Automobile Mileage/Rental	Cost of Goods Sold
50930	Cost of Goods Sold:50900 · Travel:50930 · Lodging	Cost of Goods Sold
50940	Cost of Goods Sold:50900 · Travel:50940 · Meals	Cost of Goods Sold
50950	Cost of Goods Sold:50900 · Travel:50950 · Other Travel Expenses	Cost of Goods Sold
	Expenses	Expense
55000	Fringe Benefits	Expense
55100	Fringe Benefits:55100 · Holiday Wages	Expense
55200	Fringe Benefits:55200 · Vacation	Expense
55300	Fringe Benefits:55300 · Sick Leave	Expense
55500	Fringe Benefits:55500 · Payroll Taxes	Expense
55700	Fringe Benefits:55700 · 401(k) Plan	Expense
55800	Fringe Benefits:55800 · Medical & Dental Ins	Expense

www.cakintl.com/dcaa

Sample Chart of Accounts – DCAA Compliant

Acct #	Account Name	Type
55900	Fringe Benefits:55900 · Other Employee Benefits	Expense
55910	Fringe Benefits:55910 · Insurance,Workers Comp	Expense
60000	Overhead Expenses	Expense
60100	Overhead Expenses:60100 · Conference Fees	Expense
60150	Overhead Expenses:60150 · Consultants - OH	Expense
60200	Overhead Expenses:60200 · Overhead Wages	Expense
60250	Overhead Expenses:60250 · Overhead - Bonus	Expense
60450	Overhead Expenses:60450 · Engineering Equip Purchase - OH	Expense
60451	Overhead Expenses:60451 · Lab Consumables	Expense
60500	Overhead Expenses:60500 · Product Purchase - OH	Expense
60550	Overhead Expenses:60550 · Computer Software-Eng	Expense
60700	Overhead Expenses:60700 · Travel	Expense
60711	Overhead Expenses:60700 · Travel:60711 · Airfare	Expense
60712	Overhead Expenses:60700 · Travel:60712 · Auto Mileage/Rental	Expense
60713	Overhead Expenses:60700 · Travel:60713 · Lodging	Expense
60714	Overhead Expenses:60700 · Travel:60714 · Meals	Expense
60715	Overhead Expenses:60700 · Travel:60715 · Other Travel Expenses	Expense
60702	Overhead Expenses:60702 · Meeting & Meals-OH	Expense
60900	Overhead Expenses:60900 · Overhead Allocation	Expense
70000	G & A Expenses	Expense
72000	G & A Expenses:72000 · Facilities	Expense
72200	G & A Expenses:72000 · Facilities:72200 · Facility Purchase & Maintenance	Expense
72350	G & A Expenses:72000 · Facilities:72350 · Computer/Software-Office	Expense

Sample Chart of Accounts – DCAA Compliant

Acct #	Account Name	Type
72450	G & A Expenses:72000 · Facilities:72450 · Electricity	Expense
72500	G & A Expenses:72000 · Facilities:72500 · Telephone	Expense
72520	G & A Expenses:72000 · Facilities:72520 · Internet	Expense
72600	G & A Expenses:72000 · Facilities:72600 · Other Utilties/Services	Expense
72620	G & A Expenses:72000 · Facilities:72620 · Postage and Delivery	Expense
72650	G & A Expenses:72000 · Facilities:72650 · Office Supplies	Expense
72700	G & A Expenses:72000 · Facilities:72700 · Insurance Business	Expense
72750	G & A Expenses:72000 · Facilities:72750 · Facilities Rent/Lease	Expense
72760	G & A Expenses:72000 · Facilities:72760 · Property Insurance	Expense
72770	G & A Expenses:72000 · Facilities:72770 · CAM Charges	Expense
72800	G & A Expenses:72000 · Facilities:72800 · Other Office Expenses	Expense
72820	G & A Expenses:72000 · Facilities:72820 · Property Taxes	Expense
72900	G & A Expenses:72000 · Facilities:72900 · Depreciation	Expense
74000	G & A Expenses:74000 · Finance & Administration	Expense
74200	G & A Expenses:74000 · Finance & Administration:74200 · Wages - G&A	Expense
74250	G & A Expenses:74000 · Finance & Administration:74250 · IRAD Wages	Expense
74260	G & A Expenses:74000 · Finance & Administration:74260 · IRAD Materials	Expense
74270	G & A Expenses:74000 · Finance & Administration:74270 · IRAD Professional Fees	Expense
74300	G & A Expenses:74000 · Finance & Administration:74300 · Uncompensated OT Wages	Expense
74380	G & A Expenses:74000 · Finance & Administration:74380 · Bank Service Charges	Expense

Sample Chart of Accounts – DCAA Compliant

Acct #	Account Name	Type
74400	G & A Expenses:74000 · Finance & Administration:74400 · Professional Fees	Expense
74450	G & A Expenses:74000 · Finance & Administration:74450 · Payroll Service Expense	Expense
74560	G & A Expenses:74000 · Finance & Administration:74560 · Dues and Subscriptions	Expense
74600	G & A Expenses:74000 · Finance & Administration:74600 · Credit card fees	Expense
74620	G & A Expenses:74000 · Finance & Administration:74620 · Business Mtgs/Strategy	Expense
74630	G & A Expenses:74000 · Finance & Administration:74630 · Employment Expenses	Expense
74650	G & A Expenses:74000 · Finance & Administration:74650 · Miscellaneous Expense	Expense
78000	G & A Expenses:78000 · Marketing & Sales	Expense
78100	G & A Expenses:78000 · Marketing & Sales:78100 · Marketing Expenses	Expense
78400	G & A Expenses:78000 · Marketing & Sales:78400 · Inventory for promotion	Expense
78500	G & A Expenses:78000 · Marketing & Sales:78500 · Travel/G&A	Expense
78510	G & A Expenses:78000 · Marketing & Sales:78500 · Travel/G&A:78510 · Airfare	Expense
78520	G & A Expenses:78000 · Marketing & Sales:78500 · Travel/G&A:78520 · Auto Mileage/Rental	Expense
78530	G & A Expenses:78000 · Marketing & Sales:78500 · Travel/G&A:78530 · Lodging	Expense
78540	G & A Expenses:78000 · Marketing & Sales:78500 · Travel/G&A:78540 · Meals	Expense
78550	G & A Expenses:78000 · Marketing & Sales:78500 · Travel/G&A:78550 · Other Travel Expenses	Expense
78600	G & A Expenses:78000 · Marketing & Sales:78600 · Conferences - G&A	Expense
78700	G & A Expenses:78000 · Marketing & Sales:78700 · Bid and Proposal	Expense
79000	G & A Expenses:79000 · G&A Allocation	Expense

Sample Chart of Accounts – DCAA Compliant

Acct #	Account Name	Type
80000	Unallowable Expenses	Expense
80100	Unallowable Expenses:80100 · Life Insurance	Expense
80200	Unallowable Expenses:80200 · Entertainment	Expense
80300	Unallowable Expenses:80300 · Interest Expense	Expense
80500	Unallowable Expenses:80500 · Suspense Account	Expense
80600	Unallowable Expenses:80600 · Income Taxes	Expense
80610	Unallowable Expenses:80600 · Income Taxes:80610 · Federal Tax Provision	Expense
80620	Unallowable Expenses:80600 · Income Taxes:80620 · State Tax Provision	Expense

Download this Chart of Accounts and import for any QuickBooks version except for the Online and Mac Version. These versions may require a manual entry/edit of the same.

www.cakintl.com/dcaa

NEXT STEPS ARE:

Use the provided MS Excel Chart of Accounts File and save it as an .xls or .xlsx or .csv format file. This creates an import file. An import file can be any data file that you create (usually in a spreadsheet application).

Back up your QuickBooks company file. Importing data is not reversible, so creating a backup is a good way to make sure you have a sound copy of your data should you wish to start over. Press Next.

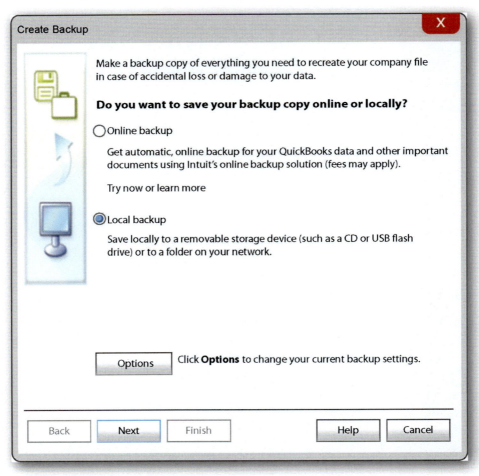

Prepare your MS Excel file for import. Must have Account Type and Name fields. The Type and Detail Type should match the types in QB. The import limit is 2 MB or 1000 rows. Use the column headings below when you prepare your file for importing account data into QuickBooks.

ACCOUNT NUMBER: The account number of the account

ACCOUNT NAME (Required): The name of an account in your chart of accounts. Note: If you're importing a child (or sub) entry for a parent (or main) entry, the parent entry must already exist in order for the child entry to be imported correctly.

ACCOUNT TYPE (Required): The type of account

Display the Import a File window under File – Utilities.

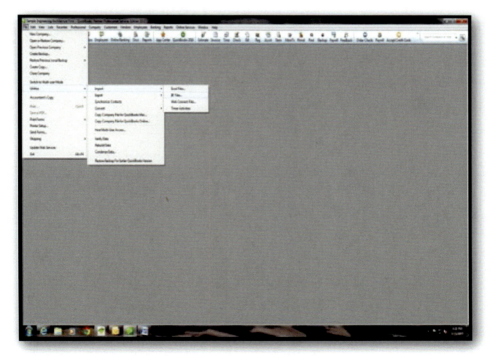

Choose Advanced Import and Select File & Sheet DCAA COA from the Downloaded file.

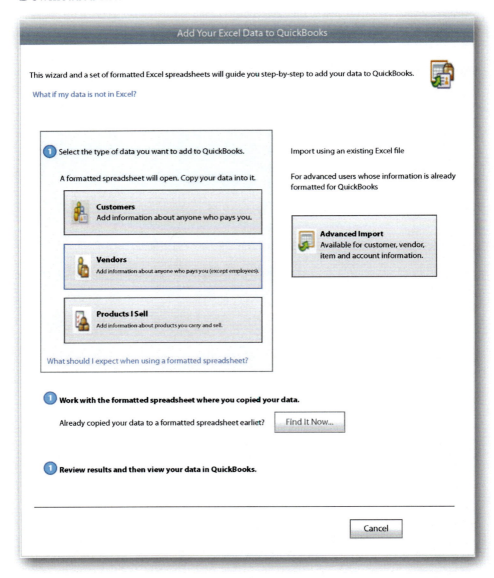

Make QuickBooks DCAA Compliant

Choose the DCAA COA sheet you just downloaded. Click Import.

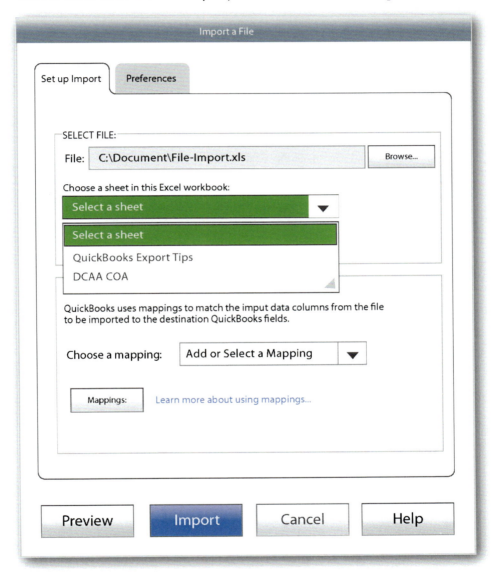

Select Add or Select a Mapping, Click Import.

Make QuickBooks DCAA Compliant

Select an import type – Choose Account. Click Save.

www.cakintl.com/dcaa

Mappings – Map QuickBooks to Import Data. Click Save.

Mapping	
Mapping name:	DCAA COA
Import type:	Account ▼

QUICKBOOKS:	IMPORT DATA:
Type	Account Type
Number	Account Number
Name	
Description	
Bank Acct. No. / Card No./Note	Account Number
As of (Date)	Account Name
	Account Type
Remind Me To Order Checks Wh...	
Track Reimbursed Exprenses	
Income account for reimb. expen...	
Is Inactive	

Save   Cancel   Help

Click the Preferences tab and specify how QuickBooks should handle errors and duplicate entries. Click Import.

For this:	Choose this:
Duplicate Handling	Prompt me and let me decide

For this:	Choose this:
Error Handling	Do not import rows with errors

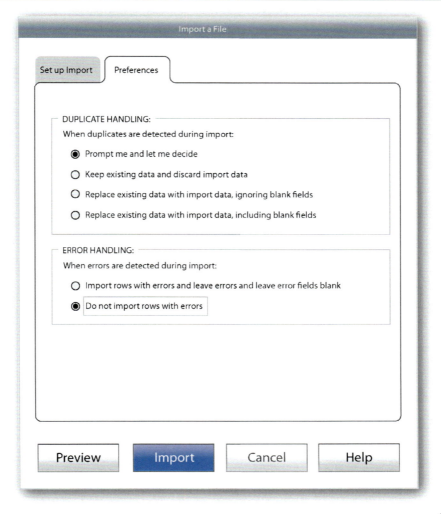

Preview the data and make any necessary corrections. Click OK.

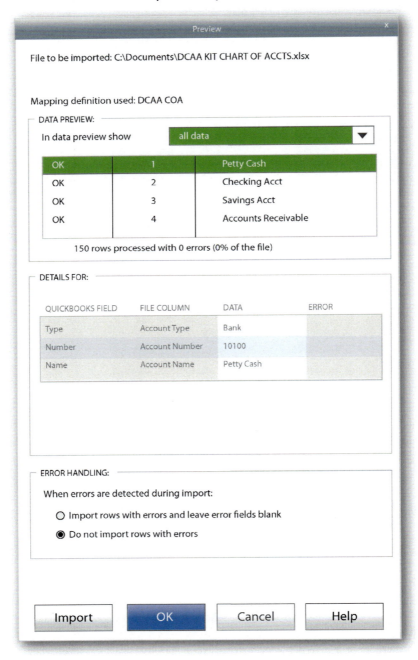

44

Make QuickBooks DCAA Compliant

The system will give you this message. Click Yes.

Choose Replace existing data with import data, ignoring blank fields. Click Apply.

If any errors occur during import, you will be prompted to save an error log. Use the error log to correct any errors. Click Save and then use the log to correct any errors.

KEY THINGS TO WATCH FOR WHILE IMPORT:

* The colon character isn't allowed, so parent/sub-account relationships will have to imported as parents first, then adjusted to become subs after the import is completed.
* Be advised that the provided Chart of Accounts is the complete final version. You will need to edit this with the necessary changes.
* If sub-accounts are imported, the parent must first exist for the sub-account to be imported. The sub accounts will not be imported.
* We have provided the sub-accounts in the listing so that you can add them manually after the import has happened. Maybe future versions of QB may accommodate them.
* The import is ADDITIVE. That means that it will add accounts to the already existing Chart of Accounts but won't subtract the standard ones.
* You can't undo this import.

- Make sure the headings in columns are: Account Number, Account Name, and Account Type.
- The Description field may not import hence it is advisable to not include it in the import. They may be reentered after the import.
- Headings are necessary, even if the column is empty or has no data.
- Entering headings should clear out any errors.
- Backup existing file prior to importing new Chart of accounts.
- If there are any current GL account numbers that match the ones being imported change them or remove them in your existing file first. Check both active & inactive accounts.

ORGANIZE YOUR NEW IMPORTED CHART OF ACCOUNTS:

- Your old accounts will not go away automatically. You need to organize them.
- Delete any old accounts that have not been used.
- Remove duplicate accounts by merging old accounts into the new imported accounts to move existing transactions from the old to the new accounts.
- Make an old account a sub-account of the new imported account, and then make the old account inactive. The existing transactions will roll up on reports and appear listed under the new account.
- Add sub-accounts from provided Chart of accounts manually.
- Merge accounts and/or Reclassify transactions by recoding to the new accounts, as necessary.
- Print a copy of the New Chart of Accounts. Also create a Memorized report for any DCAA inquiries.

www.cakintl.com/dcaa

- KEYS TO COMPLIANT DCAA CHART OF ACCOUNTS

Due to occasional version or software conflicts, you may need to manually enter the new chart from the excel version.

- * Account numbers are required by DCAA.
- * Must be sorted by account number and appear grouped together based on type.
- * The account numbers need to embed logic so that the type can be identified.
- * Do not create additional accounts to track separate contracts or projects.
- * All COGS accounts must be sub-accounts of the top-level account.
- * All expense accounts must be sub-accounts of a top-level pool account either Fringe, Overhead, G&A, Facilities, Finance & Administration, or Unallowable.

Chapter 5

ITEM LISTING

An Item in QB is anything that appears in a Form. For the sake of creating forms such as Invoices, POs. Estimates, etc. an Item is necessary. The reason you will want to use Items for DCAA compliance is that Items can also be used to track costs. From the Menu Bar go to Lists and choose Item List from drop down menu.

www.cakintl.com/dcaa

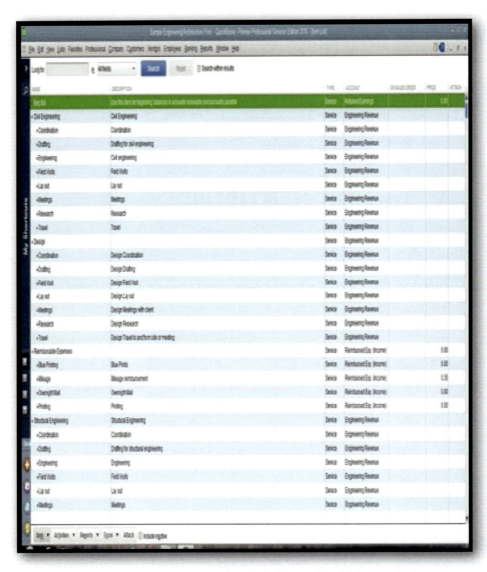

Tracking of costs with Items is rarely used, but it should be used if you want to eliminate tedious and time-consuming reconciliations to reconcile your billings to your costs, which is required for DCAA compliance.

Make QuickBooks DCAA Compliant

The Item screen ties your billings to your costs, a DCAA requirement, which requires that you can provide cost data, by unit, for each Item that is billed. At a minimum, you'll need to create an Item for each contract CLIN because funding will be entered at the CLIN level. When you record your invoices, you'll select the appropriate Items. When your record your costs, you'll select the Item that you will use when billing.

Items are built using a hierarchy, like the Customer Center, which is five levels deep. To some extent the hierarchy will mimic the set up in the Customer Center, but then branch off to provide additional billing and cost collection detail. Considerations include funding, WBS, labor categories, and CLINs.

Once the new Chart of Accounts is created, the old items will need to be re-mapped to the new relevant chart of accounts. At this point there might be a need to add or remove Items as needed. Some of the new Items are:

* Revenue Items such as Milestone billings, Cost Reimbursable billings, Fee income etc.
* Charge items such as Other Direct Costs (ODC), IR&D, Subcontracts, Overhead items etc.
* Payroll related Items such as Uncompensated Overtime

Next, set up the Items in the Item screen. You will follow the same hierarchy as in the Customer Center, but extend the list to include the contract line item number (CLIN), and the labor categories. Include the bill rate and if a staff member is a 1099 or subcontractor, set the COGS account to Direct Subcontractors. This must coincide with the Customer profile setup. See below Image on setup example:

www.cakintl.com/dcaa

. Sample Customer		Service	4000 Contract Revenue	
. Base Year		Service	4000 Contract Revenue	
. CLIN 001	Labor	Service	4000 Contract Revenue	
. Senior Engineer		Service	4000 Contract Revenue	225.00
. Engineer I		Service	4000 Contract Revenue	175.00
. Option Year		Service	4000 Contract Revenue	
. Senior Engineer		Service	4000 Contract Revenue	225.00
. Engineer I		Service	4000 Contract Revenue	175.00

Visual of Items in QuickBooks Screen:

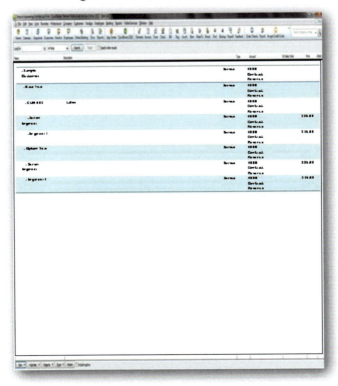

Chapter 6

CUSTOMER PROFILES

Setting up Customer profiles is key to having a smooth running system. See Policies, Procedures, & ICE in DCAA ToolKit Module 3 to learn more. Proper setup that can meet DCAA requirements for Cost accumulation also helps greatly with getting specific reports simply by setting up the projects correctly. The first thing to consider is the type of Contracts the company has or is pursuing to have.

Projects are set up in the Customer Center and the Item screen. There are two basic levels available in the Customer Center: - Customer level and Job level

Thought is important on how you will set up your projects in the Customer Center. Given that you can set up multiple levels of hierarchy in the Customer Center, you will want to consider several factors.

* Billing level is your first consideration. At which level will you create an invoice?
* The second consideration is funding. How is your contract funded?
* The third consideration is cost collection. Do you need to set up a work breakdown structure (WBS) to collect costs in a certain way to create reports?
* Your final consideration is contract line items (CLINs). Will you track your costs by CLIN at the project level, or at that line item level on an invoice?

To summarize, your basic structure in setting up a contract must address:

* Billing level
* Funding
* WBS
* CLINs

Here are some specific types of contracts and recommended set up protocols.

T&M SERVICE CONTRACTS

Time and Material (T&M) contracts are utilized to purchase labor services and incidental non-labor expenses. A fixed hourly bill rate is negotiated and the customer is billed this rate for each hour of work that is performed.

The "Material" in a T&M contract can be any other non-labor cost, such as travel or other miscellaneous expenses.

The "Material" is billed at actual costs. Occasionally, the "Material" price may be marked up with G&A and/or Fee. The fixed hourly bill rate is set for a specific labor category. For instance, a labor category of "Senior Engineer" will be billed at the contract bill rate.

T&M contracts may have multiple labor categories each with their own bill rate. Therefore, it is important to set up the labor categories in QuickBooks.

In this image, we have set up a standard federal contract with a base year and four option years. The T&M contract will have several labor categories with fixed bill rates. Each bill rate will increase in the option years. Set up the Customer Center to include a customer, and then as jobs, a contract, a base year, and four option years, in the hierarchy displayed below. See below Image on setup example:

Make QuickBooks DCAA Compliant

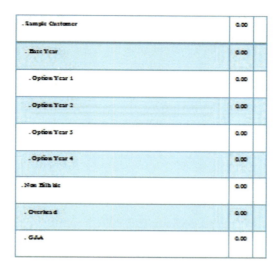

Visual of setup in QuickBooks Screen:

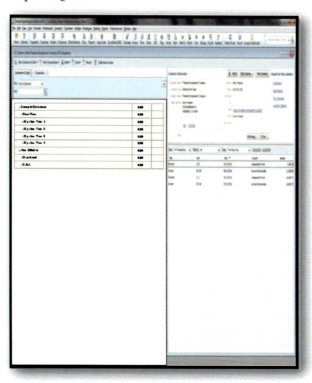

FIXED PRICE SERVICE CONTRACTS

The most common fixed price contract you'll encounter if you provide services to the federal government is one that allows you to bill a fixed monthly rate for the services you are providing. You will estimate the number of hours of service provided over the length of the contract, multiply the number of hours by the price per hour, and then divide by the number of months that you provide the service, resulting in the price you will bill each month.

Firm Fixed Price (FFP) service contracts are issued when the level of effort can be easily determined. For instance, the contract may fund one or more Full-Time Equivalents (FTEs) to provide full time support under a certain labor category.

A spin on the Fixed Price service contract is the Fixed Price Level Of Effort contract (FP/LOE). This type of contract is typically billed at a fixed monthly rate, but certain minimum levels of hours provided must be met or otherwise a price adjustment is made.

With both fixed priced and fixed price/level of effort contracts, it is wise to track hours by labor category. With FP/LOE this requirement should be obvious since your contract could be adjusted if you do not provide the minimum number of hours. For FFP contracts, the need is not as obvious, but if you were to propose a modification to increase funding, or if the federal agency proposes a modification to decrease funding, you'll need the historical labor data for negotiations.

For this reason, it is recommended that you set up your contract in the same manner as a Time & Material (T&M) contract. However, when you record your invoice, you will do so at the CLIN level, not the labor category level.

COST PLUS FIXED FEE (CPFF) CONTRACTS

Cost Plus Fixed Fee contracts are the most common type of cost-reimbursable contracts that you'll encounter in federal contracting. You may also come across Cost Plus Award Fee (CPAF), Cost Plus Incentive Fee (CPIF) and Cost Sharing (CS) contracts, which are all handled in QuickBooks in essentially the same manner.

The Customer Center is typically set up in the same manner as in the other contracts but the Item Screen, however, will be significantly different due to the manner in which cost-reimbursable contracts are invoiced. The Item Screen will need to break out the direct cost elements, the indirect pools, and the fee.

You will need to create Customer categories such as G&A, Overhead, and Unallowed for each cost pool. This way non-direct charges are also pulled as consolidations from reports. See below Image on setup example:

. Sample Customer	Service	4000 Contract Revenue	
. Base Year	Service	4000 Contract Revenue	
. CLIN 001	Service	4000 Contract Revenue	
. Direct Subcontractors	Service	4000 Contract Revenue	0.00
. Direct Material	Service	4000 Contract Revenue	0.00
. Direct Equipment	Service	4000 Contract Revenue	0.00
. Direct Travel	Service	4000 Contract Revenue	0.00
. ODC	Service	4000 Contract Revenue	0.00
. Fringe	Service	4000 Contract Revenue	0.00
. Overhead	Service	4000 Contract Revenue	0.00
. G&A	Service	4000 Contract Revenue	0.00
. Fixed Fee	Service	4000 Contract Revenue	0.00
. Non Billable	Service	4000 Contract Revenue	0.00

Visual of setup in QuickBooks Screen:

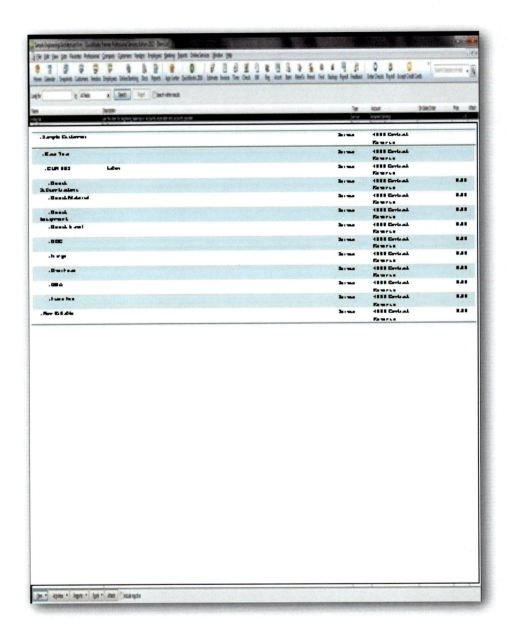

Chapter 7

PAYROLL & TIMEKEEPING

It is a DCAA requirement that the company maintain a Timekeeping system that identifies employees' labor by cost objective. Please review your current timekeeping system, identify any deficiencies and make corrections. Payroll items are set up in QuickBooks. **Please go to Policies, Procedures, and ICE in DCAA ToolKit Module 3 to get a copy of your "Make it your Own" policies.**

DCAA will evaluate your timekeeping system to ensure that it meets their requirements for accuracy and internal controls. Your timekeeping system may be "paper-based" or "electronic" but regardless of the type, the following requirements must be met:

* Daily recording of time.
* Recording all hours worked even if it is more or less than a standard 8 hour day.
* Record all paid leave.
* Record all non-billable time worked.
* All employees must record time, including executives and owners who work in the company.
* Time sheets must be signed & dated by employee.

- * Time sheets must be reviewed, signed and dated by the supervisor.
- * Corrections to time sheets must be made by the employee, and then re-signed by approver.
- * Time sheets must display the project name, charge code or paid leave account.
- * Time sheets must be approved before payroll run.
- * Time sheets must be retained until close out.

In order to use Payroll in QB the company must be running QB payroll. If third party services are used such as ADP, Paychex etc., then you can still use QB to record your payroll. In the past versions of QB and in a sample file without the payroll subscription, one can do a "mock" payroll. <u>Many so called DCAA "experts" have addressed this approach, however without the QB payroll subscription you are not able to do this any longer.</u>

Hence we will first use the standard Item List to incorporate all Payroll Items. You will need to create a payroll item for type of labor cost that you may record on a time sheet. Direct labor, Overhead labor, G&A labor, Vacation pay and Holiday pay are examples of types of labor that will require a payroll item. Be advised that Uncompensated Overtime is entered as a Deduction Payroll Item to record additional hours worked over the standard by Exempt employees. This Policy is discussed in detail in Policies, Procedures, and ICE Module 3.

Commonly required payroll items are:

- * Direct Labor
- * Overhead Labor
- * G&A Wages
- * Holiday
- * Vacation
- * Sick Time
- * Bonus

Make QuickBooks DCAA Compliant

* Jury Duty
* Garnishments
* Payroll Taxes
* Uncompensated Overtime

Payroll items link the time sheet to the general ledger accounts for labor costing. Labor distribution is the process by which labor costs are allocated to all the time that is recorded on time sheets. The distribution of labor costs must be allocated fairly among all cost objectives so that no customer or contract receives favorable treatment by receiving a cost subsidy.

DCAA will especially want to ensure that the labor costs are fairly distributed between commercial work and federal work, and between cost plus contracts and fixed price contracts. The reason for DCAA's concern is that if the labor distribution system allocates labor costs in a manner that would unfairly reduce costs applied to commercial work or fixed price contracts, it would also unfairly increase costs on federal contracts and cost plus work. The unfair share of labor costs then allocated to federal work and cost plus contracts would be incorrectly reimbursed by the federal contract, something the DCAA auditors are tasked to prevent.

QuickBooks handles the labor distribution when it runs a payroll. When a payroll is posted in QuickBooks, it creates a paycheck, which contains payroll items. They are linked to the general ledger accounts for the various types of labor, and the payroll items on the paycheck will post the labor costs to the appropriate general ledger accounts. If you run your payroll using an outside, third-party payroll provider such as ADP, you'll need to run a "mock" payroll in QuickBooks to create the labor distribution.

To run a mock payroll you will process checks by using the Write Check feature. Open a check screen and enter employee name, check date, check number, and the Net amount paid. Next enter in the memo line the pay-period information. Choose each individual payroll item for each of the labor hours recorded and map them to appropriate customer job and class codes. Payroll taxes and Uncompensated OT and any other deductions must be entered and mapped to customer projects. This process assures that each payroll check is individually recorded, allows for Bank recs etc., and also records the hours worked on each project and non-direct hours per employee as well. Example below:

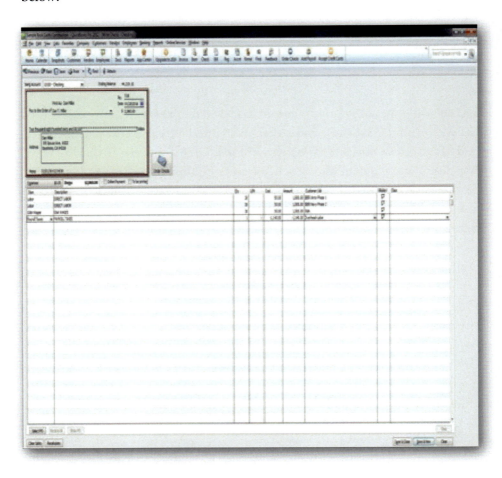

Make QuickBooks DCAA Compliant

Labor distribution reports if needed can be obtained from QB upon entry of Entering time into the Weekly time sheets. This creates a mock payroll time entry for Labor Distributions reports by using the Jobs, Time and Mileage section and generating Time reports.

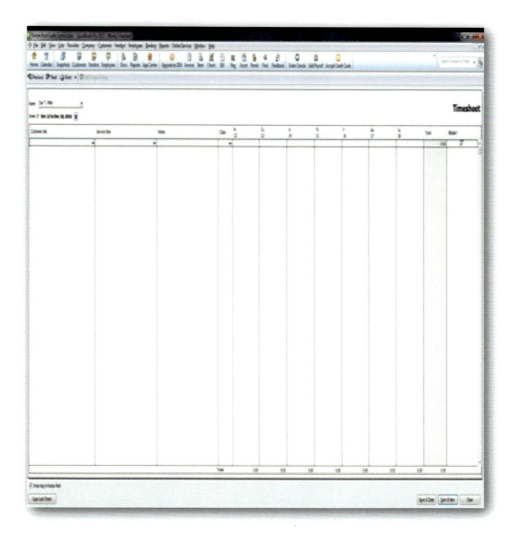

Chapter 8

INVOICING AND BOOKED VS. BILLED

CLIN SETUP AND CONTRACT FUNDING

Federal contracts are typically funded at the contract line item (CLIN) level. A CLIN is a line in your contract, typically found in Schedule B, which lists the services and products to be delivered, with a price or ceiling which cannot be exceeded. When billing the federal government, it is important to not bill in excess of funding. Your DCAA auditor will want to ensure that you have a system in place to prevent overbilling.

ENTERING CONTRACT FUNDING

- To enter your contract funding into QuickBooks, you'll need to ensure that the "Estimates" feature is enabled in QuickBooks. To enable "Estimates", navigate to the Preferences screen and then select "Job & Estimates" and select "Yes" in the box "Do you create estimates".

www.cakintl.com/dcaa

Create a New Template called Contract Budget and use the Estimates feature to create it. Open and enter the contract funding amounts by CLIN or Year as provided.

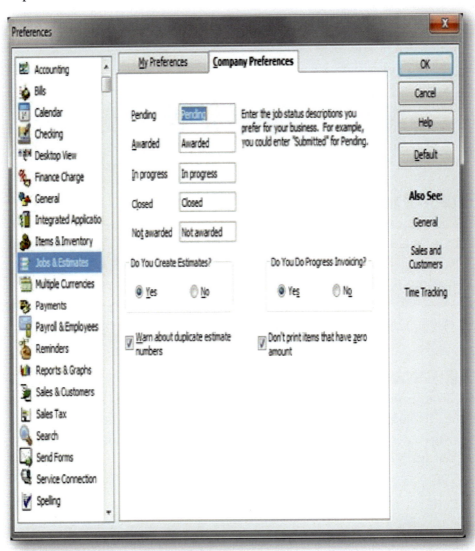

Make QuickBooks DCAA Compliant

- Open the Estimates screen in the Customer Center. Select the job that you will be funding. Set the date to the start date of the funding. Select the Items to be funding, based on your contract setup. Enter the funding amount and hours, if applicable.

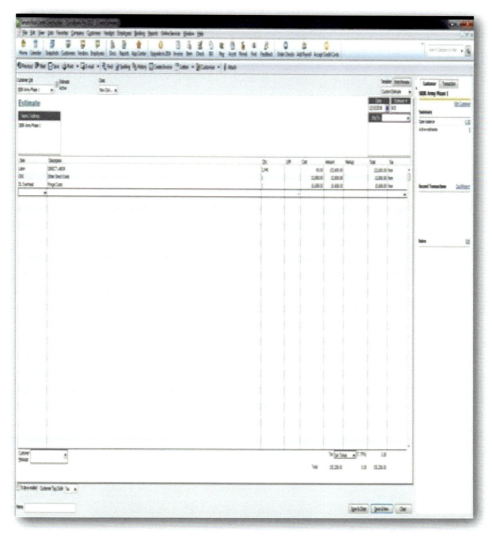

CREATING THE CONTRACT FUNDED REPORT

Open the Report "Item Estimates vs. Actuals" and modify the report by selecting all the columns for Revenue only. Change the report title to "Contract Funder Report". Memorize the report. You will use this report to track your billings versus funding.

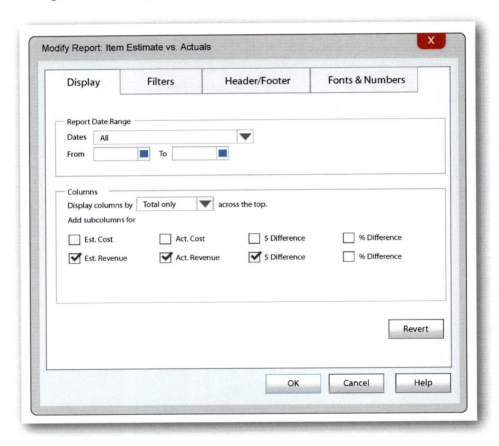

This is what the Report will look like:

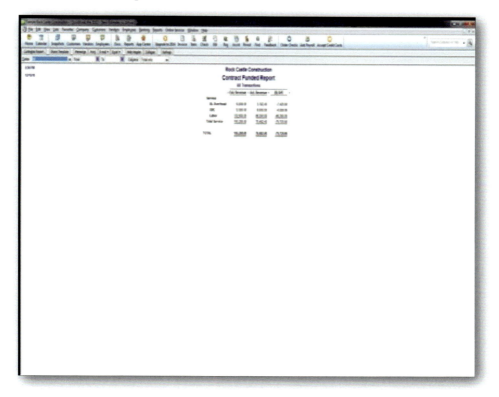

Chapter 9

ACCOUNTING BEST PRACTICES FOR COMPLIANCE

With the advent of tools such as an accounting software sometimes "conventional" wisdom of accounting tends to get ignored over software mastery.

One such area can be the case with the usage of QuickBooks or any other software for accounting. One could get so involved in the system reports & configurations that the basics of a good accounting/record keeping practice is ignored. The following pages identify areas to consider and follow as a practice to become part of creating a compliant system:

KNOWLEDGE IS KING

Accounting is a field of study requiring years of work as any other field. However sometimes business owners don't want to recognize this and try to be the accountant as well. Please seek expert counsel in getting your system **DCAA compliant** as it involves more than just some system conversions or chart of account changes.

Even though this book identifies areas that can be improved and refined, it is **Not a substitute** for a good accountant with expertise in DCAA compliance and dealing with auditors in general. It is a whole package and requires diligent accounting practices to stay compliant.

GENERALLY ACCEPTED ACCOUNTING PRINCIPLES (GAAP)

GAAP is the authority especially when it comes to DCAA compliance. Tax law based items may not pass the test. A common mistake made by business owners is to incorporate all allowed tax deductions into their accounting system. While this practice is not necessarily "incorrect" it is not always based on GAAP principle, hence it leads to Cost Transferences to federal contracts that are not allowed.

One common mistake many business owners and even CPAs, make is when it comes to Depreciation. The Section 179 allowance within the IRS tax codes based on the maximal allowed for depreciation deductions is allowed for tax purposes however should not become part of the Indirect rate calculations for Federal Contract purposes. The maximal depreciation that can be captured in a year per **GAAP** would be the only practice allowed.

PREPAID & ACCRUALS

Prepaid costs and accrual entries will need to be posted regularly and made a part of the monthly financial close. Dates are critical for accounting calculations. The same goes for all bills, invoices, payroll etc. that are posted in the system.

UNCOMPENSATED OVERTIME

This is a very important part of the Financial Statements. Please review your policy and show adherence to the same within the financial statements.

RECONCILIATIONS & DATA INTEGRITY

As a part of the compliance process, it is extremely important that your system that includes the accounting software has all reconciliations completed and current.

Reconciliations must include the following as a minimum:

Payroll: Payroll reconciliation is not only necessary for good accounting, but is a necessary component for Tax Return filings, ICE Submissions, Budgeting, and Validation of system integrity. The GL accounts must be reconciled with the Quarterly and Annual Payroll Tax Return filings. Accrual entries such as Accrued Payroll, Comp Time, Vacation Pay, Sick Pay, Holiday Pay, Payroll Tax Liabilities, Beginning & Ending Payroll Accrual balances and Uncompensated Overtime must be a part of the reconciliation.

Bank Accounts: The basic requirement. Without Bank Reconciliations there can be no other validation that can be performed. This is the first and the most critical component of all monthly close functions.

Balance Sheet: All Balance Sheet accounts must have ongoing reconciliations including Fixed Asset Roll-forwards, Taxes Payable, Depreciation Schedules, and all Equity Balances including details with Vesting schedules. All reconciliations must have supporting documentation attached such as Invoice Copies, Contract Docs, Equity Agreements, and Tax Rate Justifications etc.

AUDIT SCHEDULES & THIRD PARTY VALIDATIONS

The reconciliations must be maintained in Company Audit Schedule files that can be referred to for all audit questions with third party validations attached. This process shows a very high level of professionalism, expertise, and understanding of the accounting & audit process. DCAA & other agencies appreciate this and consider this as a sense of reliance towards the information, process, and the system at large.

www.cakintl.com/dcaa

FINANCIAL STATEMENTS

The financials statements must be in conformity to how the DCAA wishes to see them. Cost accumulation must be such that Indirect Rates can be easily identified based on Cost Pool consolidations. In QuickBooks one should be able to "collapse" the P&L and find pool costs. Further sub-ledger reports need to be run monthly and maintained.

These Financial Reports include at a minimum:

* P&L by Job. This is also referred to as the Job Cost Ledger.
* P&L by Class. This would show Business Unit costs. Important to show distinction between Government vs. Commercial business.
* Balance Sheet & P&L Consolidated. These should show at the preferred 3 Tier Cost accumulation.
* Customer/Job List – The report will detail the Job Numbers using a standard syntax and CLIN sub accounts within each Customer and Project.
* Payroll detail by Job report - The key element is that the system must be able to at a default generate reports that are first in conformity to the DCAA requirements. Then with the usage of report writers and/or customization create reports as needed for third parties, management etc. Principal system reports must be in conformity to DCAA. DCAA is checking off on a system and not just reports.

REVIEW, ANALYZE, AND UNDERSTAND

A major part of getting reports is the need to review, analyze, and understand them. So many managers and small business owners don't even look at their monthly reports, let alone take the time to understand them.

Managers need to understand what each of the Project's parameters are including if there are any cost overruns, fee hold backs, cost to complete, etc. Not only are these great management tools, they also serve as the basis for completion of other documents such as the ICE, Vouchers, Form 533M, etc.

MONTHLY CLOSE AND POST-CLOSE FUNCTIONS

* Reconcile all bank and credit card accounts.
* Verify cash entries for the period.
* Make accrual entries, reversals, and adjustments.
* Make all asset depreciation entries.
* Take physical inventory and reconcile with book inventory.
* Print financial reports.
* Issue adjustment vouchers / refunds / credits to customer agencies.
* Password protect closed month.
* Archive and back up data files.
* Export reports to Excel to calculate Indirect Rates.
* Update workbooks with Billed vs. Cost balances.

THIRD PARTY SOFTWARE AND PAYROLL INTEGRATIONS

With the advent of third party software integration to perform multiple and/or complementary functions using Payroll software, or a timekeeping software, the need for reconciling these systems is a must. One cannot have multiple systems collecting and processing data and not balance with one another.

The accounting system is the primary authority on the company's financials hence all other systems must serve as ancillary support and not ever dictate the main system reporting.

You have to work closely with payroll providers and timekeeping software companies etc. to make sure that the imported data does not corrupt the integrity of the system resident financial data.

Data mining capacity of QuickBooks to the transaction level must exist for all such transactions.

www.cakintl.com/dcaa

COMPLIANCE WITH DFARS 252.242-7006

Compliance with DFARS 252.242-7006 will apply to the Contractor's accounting system and hence requires addressing in this book. While the QuickBooks system can be refined to accommodate the main DCAA requirements, it is important that the following considerations are incorporated in the general accounting process. Only then can the system be considered compliant with the DCAA, FAR, and DFARS Requirements.

The auditors will first gain an understanding of the key processes in the accounting system related to compliance with the DFARS criteria and determine that certain controls exist and were implemented. The auditor will test those key processes and controls to determine if the contractor's accounting system complies with the system criteria in DFARS 252.242-7006.

1. DFARS 252.242-7006(c)(1) requires the contractor's accounting system to provide for a sound internal control environment, an appropriate accounting framework, and organizational structure adequate for producing accounting data that is reliable and costs that are recorded, accumulated, and billed on Government contracts in accordance with contract terms. An audit of the control environment and the contractor's compliance with DFARS Criterion 1 will be performed and the results of that audit will be incorporated in the audit and referenced.
2. Determine if the contractor's accounting system provides for identification and accumulation of direct costs by contract. (DFARS 252.242-7006(c)(3))

    a. Verify that the contractor has either a subsidiary job cost ledger or accounts receivable ledger which accumulates direct costs by contract.

3. Perform steps to verify that the contractor's system properly identifies direct costs by contract.

They will generally include:

> i. Verify that the contractor has controls in place to preclude mischarging costs of one contract to another contract.
> ii. For the significant direct costs identified during the risk assessment, trace a selection of those costs for the period covered by this audit from the accounting records through the system to documentation supporting that the costs will be identified and charged to the appropriate contract.

4. Determine if the contractor's accounting system provides for proper segregation of costs of direct costs from indirect costs (DFARS 252.242-7006(c)(2)).

    a. Verify that the contractor has controls in place to ensure proper segregation of direct cost from indirect costs.
    b. Perform a nomenclature review of accounts in the trial balance. Determine if there are any indirect accounts which appear to be of a direct nature. Determine if there are any direct accounts which appear to be of an indirect nature. Perform tests of details, if appropriate (e.g., by tracing transactions to documentation supporting that they are properly classified).

5. Analyze types of costs which are charged both direct and indirect. Those types of cost generally would have been identified in the system demonstrations. If the direct charges to fixed price contracts for a particular type of cost have decreased significantly while indirect costs have increased significantly, this may indicate that the contractor is shifting costs from fixed price contracts to indirect pools which would result in mischarging to flexibly price contracts. Perform tests of details, if appropriate.

6. Determine if the contractor's accounting system provides for a timekeeping system that identifies employees' labor by intermediate or final cost objective (DFARS 252.242-7006(c)(9)).

a. Verify that labor is charged to intermediate and final cost objectives based on timekeeping documents (paper or electronic timecards) completed and certified by employees and approved by the employees' supervisors.
b. Verify that the contractor has segregation of duties and responsibilities in its timekeeping system (e.g., division of duties between personnel responsible for preparation of time and attendance records, and those responsible for the preparation and distribution of the payroll.)

7. Determine if the contractor's accounting system provides for a labor distribution system that charges direct and indirect labor to the appropriate cost objectives (DFARS 252.242-7006(c)(10)).

The majority of the work for this criterion would be accomplished during the floor check(s) for the period covered by the audit. However, as a part of the observations and inquiry during the walk-through for the audit, it would be verified and documented that the contractor has controls in place to ensure the labor distribution system charges direct and indirect labor to the appropriate cost objectives. (For example, the contractor should have demonstrated its procedures and controls related to the accumulation and recording of labor cost to cost objectives. These procedures should include controls over the issuance of work authorizations and provide for work descriptions that are sufficiently detailed to track the effort to the appropriate intermediate or final cost objective and to identify the effort as allowable, unallowable, direct or indirect.) For example, the auditor might:

* Use the information obtained during the risk assessment procedures (e.g., walkthroughs) to assist in identifying high risk areas.
* Evaluate labor distribution documents for the period covered by this audit to identify employees charging labor effort to the identified risk areas.
* Select a sample of employee labor charges from the labor distribution report and request the applicable timesheets.

- Trace the labor hours and job numbers reflected in the labor distribution report to the selected timesheets.
- Trace employee hourly rates reflected in the labor distribution report to payroll records.
- Verify the labor cost distribution records reconcile to the cost accumulation records in labor subsidiary and to the general ledger accounts, if applicable.
- Using the timesheets obtained above, compare the job numbers on the timesheets to the applicable work authorization documents.
- Verify that the work authorizations are in sufficient detail to determine the appropriate cost objective and if the cost is allowable or unallowable and should be charged direct or indirect.

These are examples; however, auditors will perform the necessary procedures in the circumstances to determine compliance with the criterion.

8. Determine if the contractor's accounting system provides for the accumulation of costs under general ledger control (DFARS 252.242-7006(c)(5) and reconciliation of subsidiary cost ledgers and cost objectives to the general ledger (DFARS 252.242-7006(c)(6)).

   a. Determine if the contractor maintains a chart of accounts which is updated in a timely manner.
   b. Verify that the contractor's policies and procedures require that job cost ledger and other books of account are reconciled and currently posted to the general ledger control accounts.
   c. Selectively test the contractor's reconciliations for the period covered by this audit to verify that the subsidiary cost ledgers and cost objectives reconcile to the general ledger accounts. If this is a computerized function, selectively test to verify that it is occurring properly.
   d. Obtain evidence that costs from the job cost ledger and other books of account have been regularly posted to the general ledger control accounts for the period covered by this audit.

9. Determine if the contractor's accounting system provides for approval and documentation of adjusting entries (DFARS 252.242-7006(c)(7)).

   a. Verify that the contractor has controls in place to ensure that adjusting entries are properly approved and documented. This should include a division of duties between personnel responsible for authorizing journal entries and those responsible for posting journal entries in the ledger.
   b. Test a selection of adjusting entries (e.g., correcting, transferring, closing, and credit) for the period covered by the audit to verify that they were appropriately approved and that the basis for the adjustment was adequately documented.
   c. For any unusual or sensitive items identified in the step above that warrant further review, request and review information from the contractor to determine if the adjustments are appropriate.

10. Determine if the contractor's accounting system provides for management reviews or internal audits of the system to ensure compliance with the contractor's established policies, procedures, and accounting practices (DFARS 252.242-7006(c)(8)).

    Note: The contractor's monitoring of its accounting system should include considering whether controls are operating as intended and that they are modified as appropriate for changes in conditions. The contractor's monitoring process may include, in addition to management reviews or internal audits, other forms of monitoring such as personnel performing similar activities and can be accomplished through ongoing monitoring activities (which are built into the contractor's normal recurring activities), separate evaluations, or a combination of the two.

    a. Determine if the contractor's policies and procedures require management reviews/monitoring of its accounting system and that the timeframes and/or guidelines appear sufficient given the complexity and size of the contractor's operations to determine that controls are operating as intended and that they are modified as appropriate.

b. Evaluate management review and other monitoring activities for the period covered by the audit to determine if the contractor is performing reviews in accordance with time frames and guidelines established in the policies and procedures.

11. Determine if the contractor's accounting system provides for interim (at least monthly) determination of costs charged to a contract through routine posting of books of account (DFARS 252.242-7006(c)(11)).

    Obtain evidence that, for the period covered by the audit, the contractor determined and recorded costs to contracts at least monthly (generally to the job cost ledger).

12. Determine if the contractor's accounting system provides for a logical and consistent method for the accumulation and allocation of indirect costs to intermediate and final cost objectives (DFARS 252.242-7006(c)(4)).

    Verify that the contractor indirect rate structure is formally documented, with a written description of the make-up of pools and bases.

13. Determine if the contractor's accounting system provides for cost accounting information as required to readily calculate indirect cost rates from the books of accounts (DFARS 252.242-7006(c)(15ii)).

    a. Verify that interim and final indirect expense rates can be readily calculated from the books of accounts.
    b. Verify that, for the period covered by this audit, the contractor provided timely provisional indirect rates (both billing and forward pricing, if applicable) and monitored the rates for any significant variances.

14. Determine if the contractor's accounting system provides for exclusion from costs charged to Government contracts of amounts which are not allowable in terms of FAR Part 31, Contract Cost Principles and Procedures, and other contract provisions (DFARS 252.242-7006(c)(12)).

a. Verify that the contractor has controls in place to ensure unallowable costs are identified and excluded from costs charged to Government contracts (FAR 31.201-6).
b. Verify that the detail and depth of records maintained by the contractor as backup support for proposals, billings, or claims are adequate to establish and maintain visibility of identified unallowable costs, including directly associate unallowable costs.
c. Perform procedures to test the contractor's controls for identifying and excluding unallowable costs from costs charged to Government contracts. Work performed in and the results of other recently completed audits (e.g., audits of price proposals or incurred costs) will be used to the extent possible. For example, if those audits have identified significant costs that are not allowable under FAR Part 31, consider whether, in the given circumstances, this indicates that the contractor's system fails to comply with this criterion, especially if the costs are expressly unallowable.

15. Determine if the contractor's accounting system provides for identification of costs by contract line item and by units (as if each unit or line item were a separate contract) if required by the contract (DFARS 252.242-7006(c)(13)).

Verify for a selection of contracts that during the period covered by the audit the contractor's system accumulated and identified costs at the requisite level of detail as specified in the contract terms and conditions (e.g., by contract line item and units if required by the contract).

16. Determine if the contractor's accounting system provides for segregation of pre-production costs from production costs (DFARS252.242-7006(c)(14)).

Verify that pre-production costs are routinely segregated from production costs to assist in re-pricing or follow-on contract pricing (applies primarily to manufacturing costs).

17. Determine if the contractor's accounting system provides for cost accounting information as required by contract clauses concerning limitation of cost (FAR 52.232-20), limitation of payments (FAR 52.232-22), or allowable cost and payment (FAR 52.216-7) (DFARS 252.242-7006(c)(15i)).

18. Determine if the contractor's accounting system provides for billings that can be reconciled to the cost accounts for both current and cumulative amounts claimed and comply with contract terms (DFARS 252.242-7006(c)(16)).

    a. Verify that the contractor's system produces cost information at a sufficient level of detail for use in pricing follow-on contracts.
    b. Verify that the contractor's cost accounting system in accordance with the Generally Accepted Accounting Principles.

MORE FROM CAK INTERNATIONAL, LLC

With both Multi-State and Multinational offices CAK delivers DCAA compliance solutions even at a localized level through Audit Representations, System Conversions, Expert Consultations, and Support Teams. This collective DCAA Toolkit (3 Modules) contains proven, actual, and real time valuable insights that can be incorporated to achieve and maintain DCAA compliance.

For additional information on all our offered services, contact us at:

(866) 367-2256 Phone
(877) 367-2257 Fax
solutions@cakintl.com E-Mail
www.cakintl.com

Made in the USA
Middletown, DE
31 December 2016